HEALING VIBES

IT'S ABOUT HEALING GRACEFULLY

TANIA

ISBN 979-888606618-0

"DEDICATED TO MY GRANDPA AND GRANDMA

MR. KARNAIL SINGH MRS. KANTA DEVI "

ALWAYS IN MY HEART

Contents

Contents

JAI MATA DI

Foreword

Here is a bouquet of multifarious flowers, gathered from the garden of life and wrapped in poetic garb as a meaningful gift to the reader.

Here is a collection of poems composed by the author at different times and in different situations in different states of mind, bound together in one common thread running through all of them. As the name suggests "Healing vibes" it's about healing gracefully in which the author wants to make people realise their will to tackle difficult situations of life just only by holding their strong inner faith. Sometimes situations are not accordingly we want so in that situation never feel depressed. Here is just an attempt by the author to make people realise the beauty of healing through poetry.

Preface

My book "Healing vibes....It's about healing gracefully" is like a beautiful collage of one's feelings and emotions. We, people, get easily depressed by certain bad experiences that we came across in our life. This is an attempt to heal people from the dilemma through my poetry. As I spend an immense amount of my energy trying to understand others. I can listen to their story and in my mind write myself into their experience. Weaving myself together with their story, I can create a new character that feels authentic. Often, I find myself feeling their emotions. This skill allows writing to come naturally for me, but it does take a mental toll. In my daily life, I would like to offer support to those in need, however, I am able. Through my writing, I hope to inspire and touch other people in the ways that I feel inspired through my understanding of others' struggles. I believe that compassion creates endless opportunities for spreading a message of hope and love.

I HOPE YOU ENJOT IT!

1. Healing Vibes

Let's carry our troubles with dignity ; like a rose carries her thorns.
The rose, she knows ~ without accepting the thorns as part of herself, she won't be able to heal.
We are her, all of us.

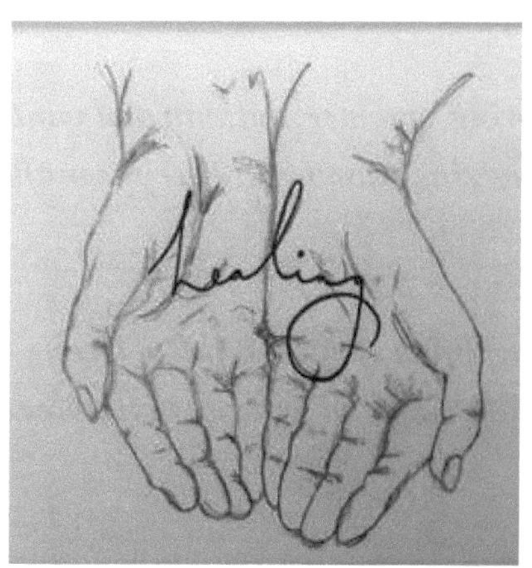

LET'S HEAL GRACEFULLY

2. Nature's Message

I am nature,
The one God's creature.

Sinking down by your cruel bounds,
No one like you ever founds.

Spring, summer ,autumn and winter,
Amazing seasons felt every year after.

Think of a forest full of trees,
Fluttering and dancing in the breeze.

They are all burning out,
Mountains are also in doubt.

Whether we mould into a road ,
Or get ready for erode.

The birds that soar high in the sky,
Are on the verge of die.

Oh! Brutal man,
Harm me as much as you can.

Now I show you my aggressive form,
An intolerable and belligerent storm.

That day is soo near,
When you all trap in a fear.

Regrets bounds you all around,
With the tag of sinner you crowned.

So, before the time fades away,
Step in the right way.

Protect what has been given for free
The waters, skies, wildlife and trees.

3. Sometimes Thought

Sometimes I wonder why?
I always wanted to fly
For me to reach the sky
And to feel being on high

I dream to be on top
That's why I never stop
Like a ballon waiting to flop
Like a tear waiting to drop

I will continue
To witness a nice view
Even the winds wants me to blew
I will still let my dreams grew

Who know what tomorrow brings
Just let your heart sings
Never stop spreading your wings
Just think , here you are the only king.

4. Why?

Why to live in despair?
When it's right time to take away fear.

Why to blame yourself?
When it's time to refine oneself.

Why to always feel annoyed?
When a smile makes us satisfied.

Why to always feel panic?
When everything surrounds us is organic.

Why to always consider rejection?
When one is following right direction.

Why to always bother about past?
When worst experience is already lost.

Why to always Abandon night?
When a night is always responsible for a new day's light.

TANIA

5. Soul

"In a world where everyone wears a mask,

it's a privilege to see a soul ".

6. It's Her Day

Bringing in me the best of mine,
Along with her seems everything fine.

More than a friend I found in her.,
Glory of her love makes my sorrows blur.

Being my supporter in all bad turns,
Nourishing me with her love and concerns.

Admiring her for her boundless love,
For me she is my gift from above.

As we journey throughout this life
She will find me by her side.

From my heart to her soul,
Wishing her a happiest birthday full of bowl.

7. My Destination

Strong enough
to bear all pain,
Am all alone
walking in the lane.

Found many ups and downs
on my way,
In the praise of troubles
what can I say?

Not easy
to reach the destination,
Unless
we are in a competition.

With the desire
to achieve success,
Only work hard
and worry less.

Being alone,
we fall and rise,

But in every situation
always remember to be wise.

Not everyone
here is alike,
Some are here to appreciate
and some are for dislike.

8. Smile

Smile to the trees,
Smile to the sea,
I smile to everything,
I see around me.

Smile to the leaves,
Smile with the beats,
Smile on your victory,
From all the thieves.

Smile is a gift,
A gift to shift,
Bad days to good days,
And sadness will drift.

Smile not to gain,
But smile to regain,
The happiness you lost,
The smile is its cost.

9. My Poetry

Your silence spills into my poetry,

SLEEPLESS ~

Wandering in my dreams without poetry.

10. Best From Worst

My past teaches me soo well,
So that I can happily dwell.

That time was little bit worst,
But the experiences that I gain were best.

We all have to face some phases in our life,
Which displays the fact that we are alive.

Our mistakes reveals that we are trying,
At each time with a new step we are growing.

May be our target seems so far,
And our heart filled with many scar.

But it's our battle so only we have to face,
Only the lane of success we have to chase.

Obstacles are always on our way,
Only with our hard work they can turn away.

Success not lies in achieving every goal,

Success lies in our every step that leads us towards our goal.

Make our last meeting
As that was our first like
After I die,
Don't cry.
This is the turning point of your life
When u have to manage
Everything without mine
So don't get panic and
Turns out everything right
Because
We will meet again in our next life
Until then,
U will find me in the stars above the sky.
So my love
After I die
Don't cry.
With the hope that
As like those love birds
We again fly.

13. No

No is enough beacuse;
Is a complete sentence.
It does not require justification or explanation.

14. It's Never Late

It's not too late
So get up fast don't wait
Maybe I will fail
But I will continue to sail
Even if I see no gain
I will try again
I may drown in pain
But I won't cry in vain
I will keep trying again
By following the perfect lane
Finally then i reach at end of the line
Where everything seems perfect and fine

15. If

If you wants to try,
Then try something good.

If you wants to help,
Then help in a selfless way.

If you wants to say,
Then say in a polite way

If you wants to love,
Then love someone unconditionally.

If you wants to enhance,
Then enhance your knowledge.

If you wants to pray,
Then pray for others too.

If you wants to spread,
Then spread happiness around.

If you wants to protest,

Then protest for your rights.

If you wants to reject,
Then reject all the evils.

If you wants to leave,
Then leave your all worries.

If you wants to keep,
Then keep everyone with you.

16. Peace

Go for a 4 hour walk
Into the forest.
Without any make up,
In comfy clothes.
Go hug a random tree,
Feel it's heartbeat.
Observe all the bugs.
Observe the flowers,
Don't pluck them.
Sit still and watch
How animals react to your aura.
Go swim in
Lakes, rivers or the seas.
Walk barefoot on the earth.
Learn to be one with nature,
By being at peace with your
Own nature.

17. Go With The Flow

If one way doesn't work, we try another way.
If one path doesn't lead to our destination, we try another path.
So why do we often stick to the things which hurt us,
Let them go and let us simply
"Go With the Flow"

18. Let It Be

The time I spent with you,
Gave me a hope and disappointment too.

I never thought that this day would come in our life,
As like everyone here is not alike.

My heart has no more desire,
Because nothing left in our love to admire.

Life has many ups and downs,
Happiness always fade all our wounds .

Many people come and go,
Who will be with us till end we don't know.

Everything happens only for a reason,
Like year follows every season.

Being upset for past is of no use,
So a strong belive for oneself should never loose.

Determination to achieve desires is always right,

In order to make future bright.

So, let's make everything else easy,
By letting away things which makes us griefy.

19. Like You And Me

Like a Parrot
in the cage
Like a Beam
stands with courage
Like a River
that flowing
My love for u
is continue growing

Like the Birds
that fly
Like the clouds
thundering in the sky
Like the Seasons
that change
I am yours and you are mine
at every age

Like a Heart
that beats
Like a Sugar
as sweet

Like a Dream
that comes true
I feel so special
only with you.

Like those
Shining stars
Like those
Blooming flowers
Like a night
that brings a new day
Thank you for loving me
I only want to say

20. Flamboyant

I paint my life in shades of black,
to omit cracks left on my track.

So no one sees the pain I hide,
stuck deep inside, my solemn guide.

Miracle happens for sure one day,
That grasp me to the right way.

Chase all my worries and let them go,
My inner faith never gets low.

Then I add some white, my days turn grey ,
balanced displays, hope peace could stay.

Merging black and white new colours display,
Darkness of my life in this way fades away.

21. Universe

"If there is happiness for me to receive,its only because you kept me here".

22. As Like

As like struggle is the key to success,
Only with hardwork you can progress.

As like a smile is the jewel of face,
Happiness will turn your dark nights into days.

As like a rose is the gift of nature,
We should appreciate God's every creature.

As like a river always finds it's way,
So think twice before you say.

As like everything happens for a reason,
Your worst time passes like a season.

As like a new day came after every night,
Your struggle makes your future bright.

23. That Fine Day

In the break of day,
I was on the way.

To reach the garden full of flowers,
Where I spend my precious hours.

Yesterday it was raining all night,
But a new dawn made everything bright.

Here the spring is fresh and every leaf is new,
The grass beneath is also wet with dew.

After I reach , I saw something unique,
Which fascinated me towards it complete.

Encircled by some green leaves,
Out of which a glimpse of beauty reveals.

A beautiful rose was standing alone,
With bright red petals that always shone.

As the sun starts rising it's shine,

Everything seems perfect and fine.

24. Alone

Few questions are bouncing in my mind,
Their answers are very difficult to find.

I am lost in my own world,
In which my happiness is blurred.

Sometimes I just feel little depressed,
Just wanna take a break and rest.

Then in the dark night I feel so alone,
While remembering all my battles that I never won.

This scatters a wave of disappointment around,
And I again left alone with my tears and wounds.

25. One Step Forward

According to me
"Hard work + patience = satisfaction"
To achieve something is not success Your every step towards your goal is your actual success.
With your every step you can feel that satisfaction.

26. My Mom

My day begins with her smiling face,
Without her assist my life has no base.
Loving her is my only desire,
Take her into the glory of admire.
Her selfless service for mine,
Endure me into the world of shine.
As, only with her genuine deeds,
On the lane of success I leads.

27. Mother Earth

Everyday we get nature's gift for free
Just think about all the beauty we see

The song of a bird and flowers that bloom
The peace we find at dawn in our room!

The gift of nature is always there
Start seeing it and you will love , I swear

Don't you think we should keep it safe

So, LET'S TAKE A PLEDGE ON THIS EARTH DAY……..

TO KEEP IT CLEAN AND GREEN IN EVERY WAY….

28. More Than Words

Poetry is more than words
It is a creation
Of feelings from one's heart
A celebration of life and love
It is healing for the broken
Hope for the hopeless
An expression of a mood
Poetry is a universal language
It is you, it is me
It is everything we are meant to be
It is real, but also a fantasy
Poetry is art... music... a story...
So...

When you are reading poetry
Read it out loud
Read it slowly
Read it again
And again
And again

And you will feel
And you will see
The magic
That is poetry

29. Don't Quit

I love my life
I love my way

Out of many obstacles
I found my way
I never bother what others say

I give my best
To achieve the best
I never stop trying
And get the success

Mistakes follow me in every step
With some patience,
I have to accept
Only through struggle dreams come true
It's your life
So only you have to do

30. It's Love?

Whenever we say; I felt loved
We are actually saying; I felt accepted

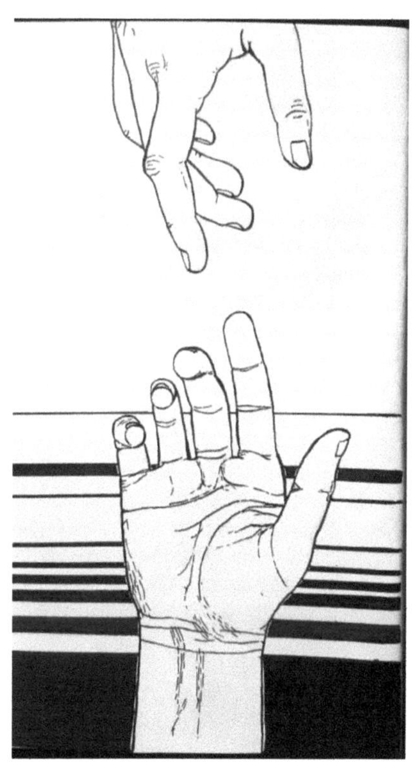

31. Her Presence

The glittering rays of the sun,
Dancing in her bun.
The white pearls studded in the blue sky,
Signifies the beauty of her eyes.
That smoothly flowing sea waves,
Mark every step she takes.
The gentle breeze blowing around,
Produces a pleasant sound.
The melody of the swooping birds,
Welcome her with their cheering words.

32. Wandering Thoughts

His pacifying presence
feels like a warm breeze
that gently calms my eyes,
calms my soul and
soon slows down
the noise around.
His crooning satisfied my ears.
Suddenly
I felt something on my hand
and I was like
wow.! It's a drop of rain that gives me inner peace.
Now a wave of love
spreads far and wide
and your presence
finally makes
everything bright.
Eventually,
I slowly opened my eyes
and realized that
it was a beautiful dream
that I was lost in.
although it was a dream

But it seems to be
one of the best moments
of my life

33. Roses

Hidden in the shadows,
a beauty no one knows,
yet still it grows,
The Unseen Rose.

One day the unseen rose will bloom,
the petals will unfold,
revealing secrets untold,
beauty to behold.

34. Rosa woodsii / Woods Rose

I commonly called as
North American Wildflower rose.
My five light to dark pink petals
Surrounding yellow stamen as shown.
I am fast-growing
And long-lived rose.
U can find me in
Meadow edges and all forest across.
I support both
Pollination and bird populations.
Please support me
By enhancing my generations.

35. China Rose

I have a
small, shrubby shape
With beautiful large flower.
My silky petals
Changes it's colour
throughout each Bloom's life
Yellow transaction to pink
And ends in a deep crimson.
I am the result of
intense hybridization in Chinese garden
So, my beauty deserve all
Your attention.
If anything else
U love in me
Please mention.

36. Alba Rose

I am tall and classic
Also known as the
"White roses of shakespeare".
With dark blue-green leaves
and fewer thrones.
As due to my grand heights
I provide a beautiful backdrop
to other plants.
I double blooms with
gorgeously apricot coloured petals
deepen to a
richer pink in the centre.
Additionally I give off
a musk of myrrh.
So you can feel
Like true royalty.

37. Damask Rose

U will find me
In the middle East.
I signifies both
Beauty and fragrance
That resides me.
I provide u all those
Delicious rose-flavoured treats
And indulgent spa products.
I also extracted my scent
to make
Rose essential oils, rose water
And rose flavouring products.
My 40 pink petals
wrap each other.
So,please don't pluck me
Otherwise
U will lose me forever.

38. Gallicas Rose

I commonly called as
Old garden rose.
I initially bred by
The Greeks and Romans.
I am smaller in stature,
So, if you don't have much garden room,
I am a great choice for you,
From the nature.
My delicate
Pink layer of petals,
Create a lush around the
creamy white centre.
My fragrance
Refreshes you all
My beauty too
Fascinates you all

THANK YOU FOR BEING PART OF THIS JOURNEY WITH ME.......I HOPE YOU ENJOY READING THIS BOOK.

Printed by Libri Plureos GmbH in Hamburg,
Germany